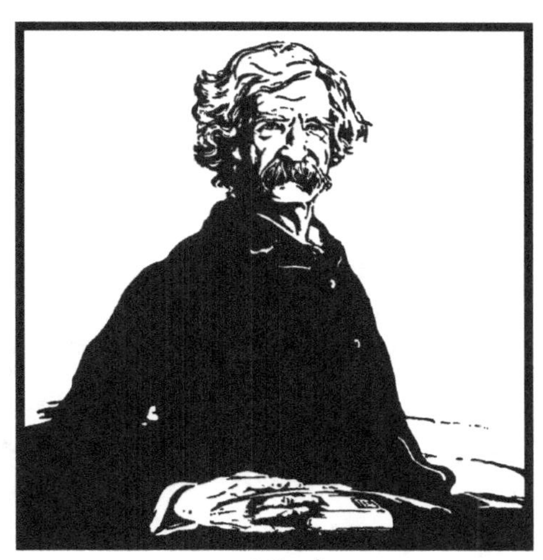

Mark Twain

Calendar & Character

By William Nicholson

Copyright ©2014 Velluminous Press

The owner of this book is granted permission to scan or photocopy the included images,
and to use these scans or copies in finished commercial or non-commercial products.
All other rights, including the right to offer these images as stock images, are reserved.

Original lithographs translated by Holly Ollivander.

ISBN: 978-1-905605-44-6

www.velluminous.com

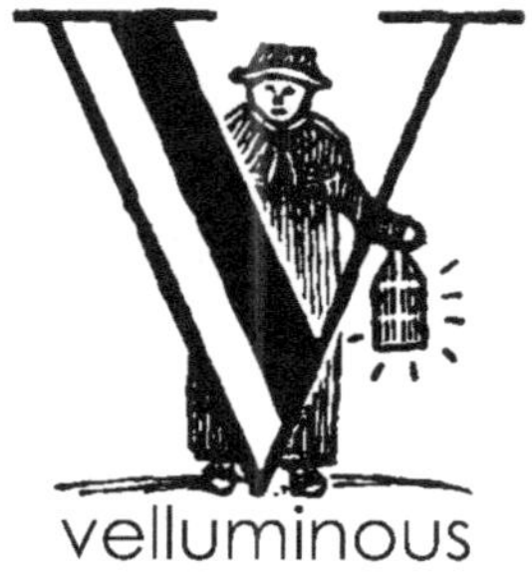
velluminous

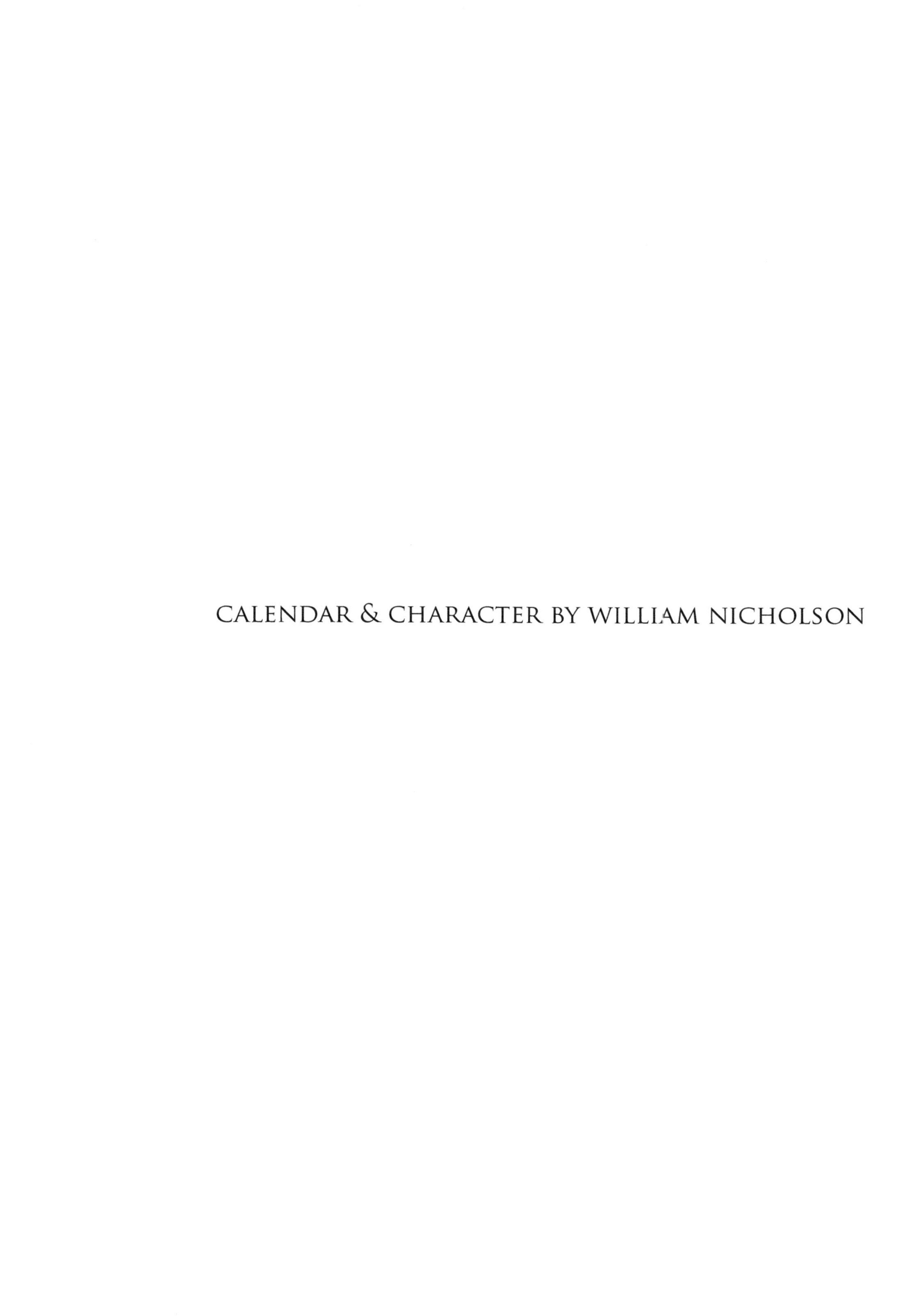

CALENDAR & CHARACTER BY WILLIAM NICHOLSON

William Nicholson (5th February 1872 – 16th May 1949) was a painter, engraver, graphic artist, stained glass craftsman, author, illustrator and theatre set designer with an astonishing gift: he pursued light and pinned down shadow with a visual brevity and mastery rarely seen in Western Art. The images within this book still stand as an exemplar of how to distil the essence of three dimensions into two colours, proving a continual inspiration to generations of graphic artists since.

It is our pleasure to present, in a scanner-friendly printed format, the following images as Nicholson originally saw them, and before time and pigment altered them forever.

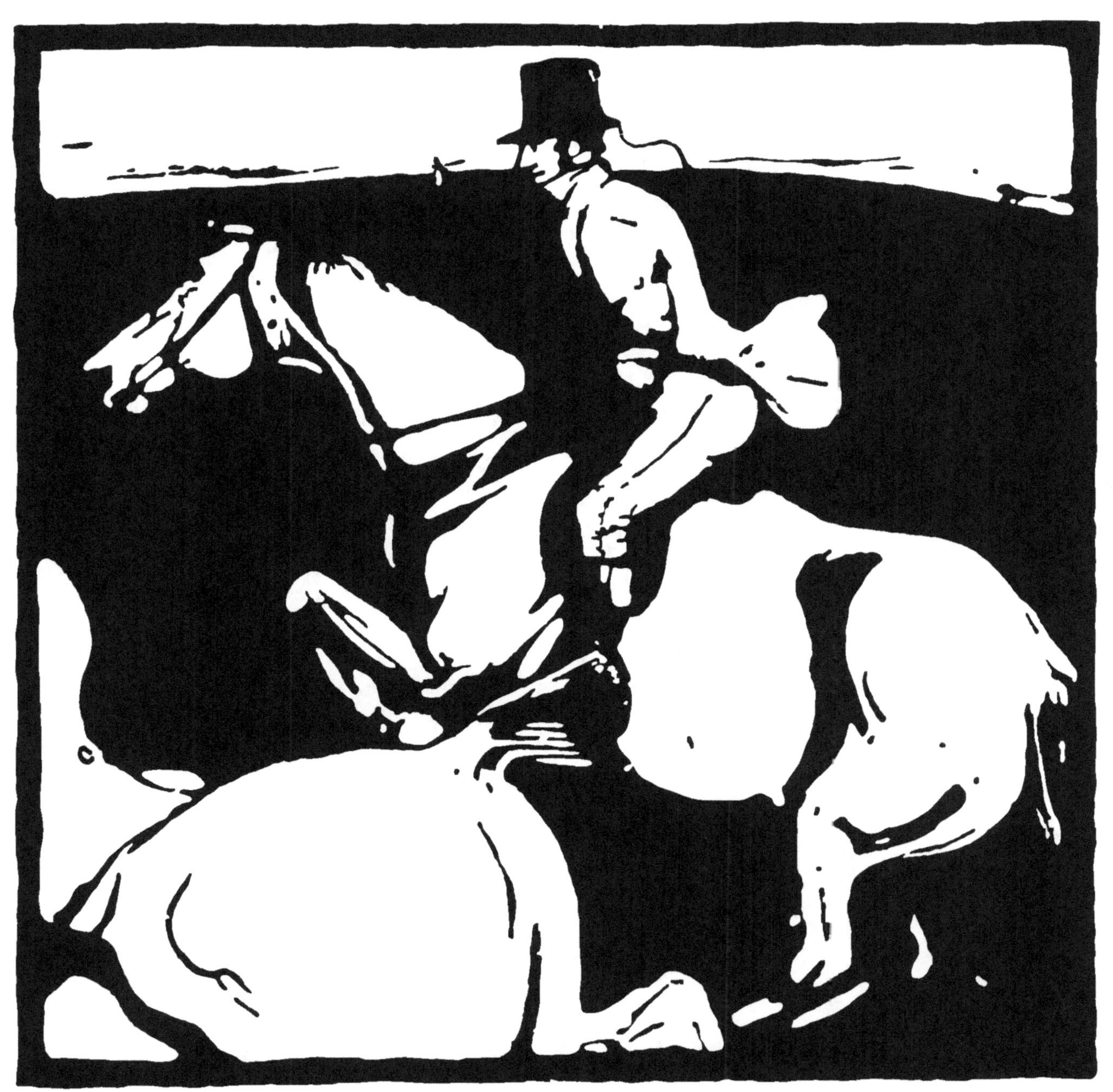

January.

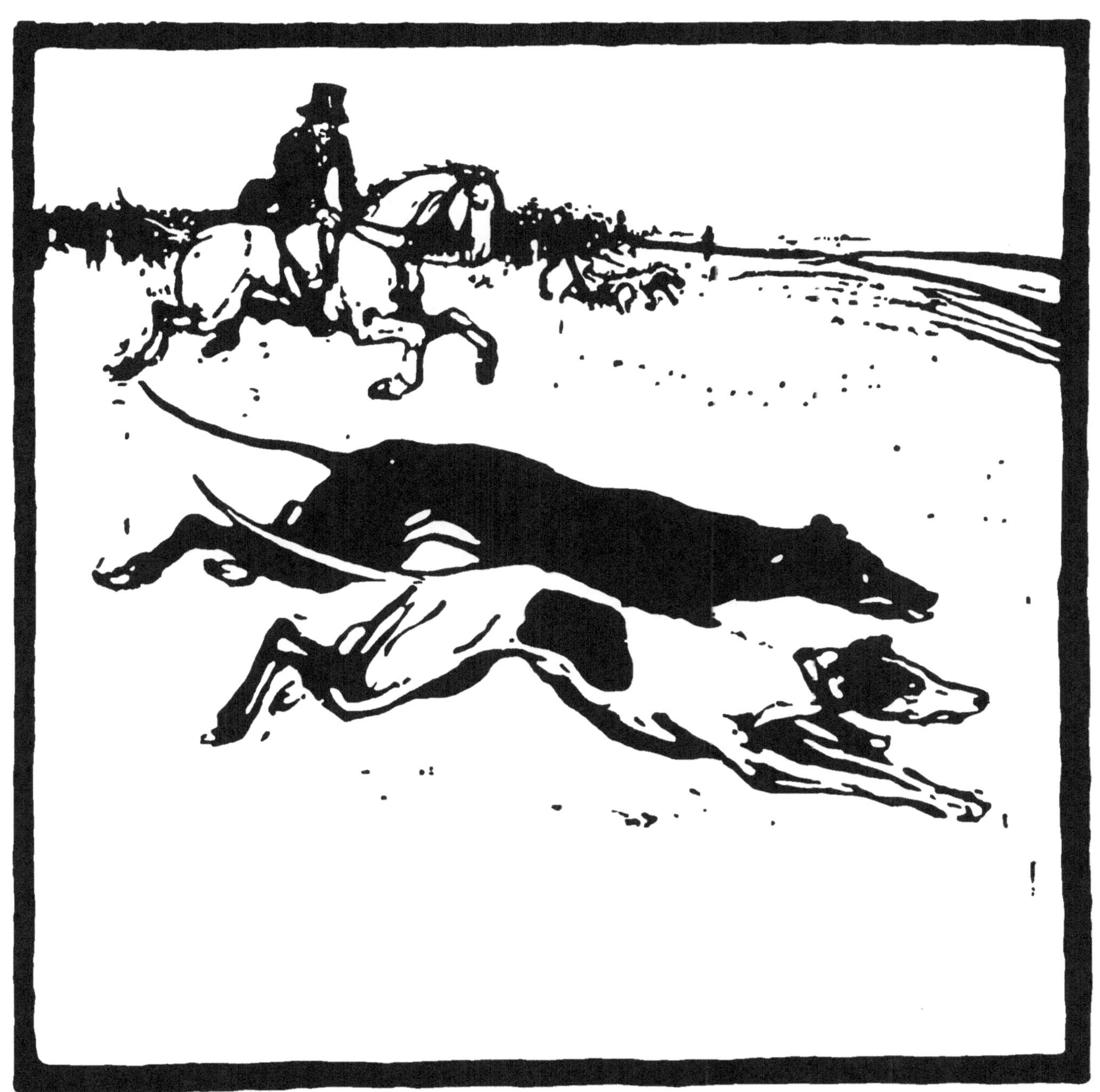

February.

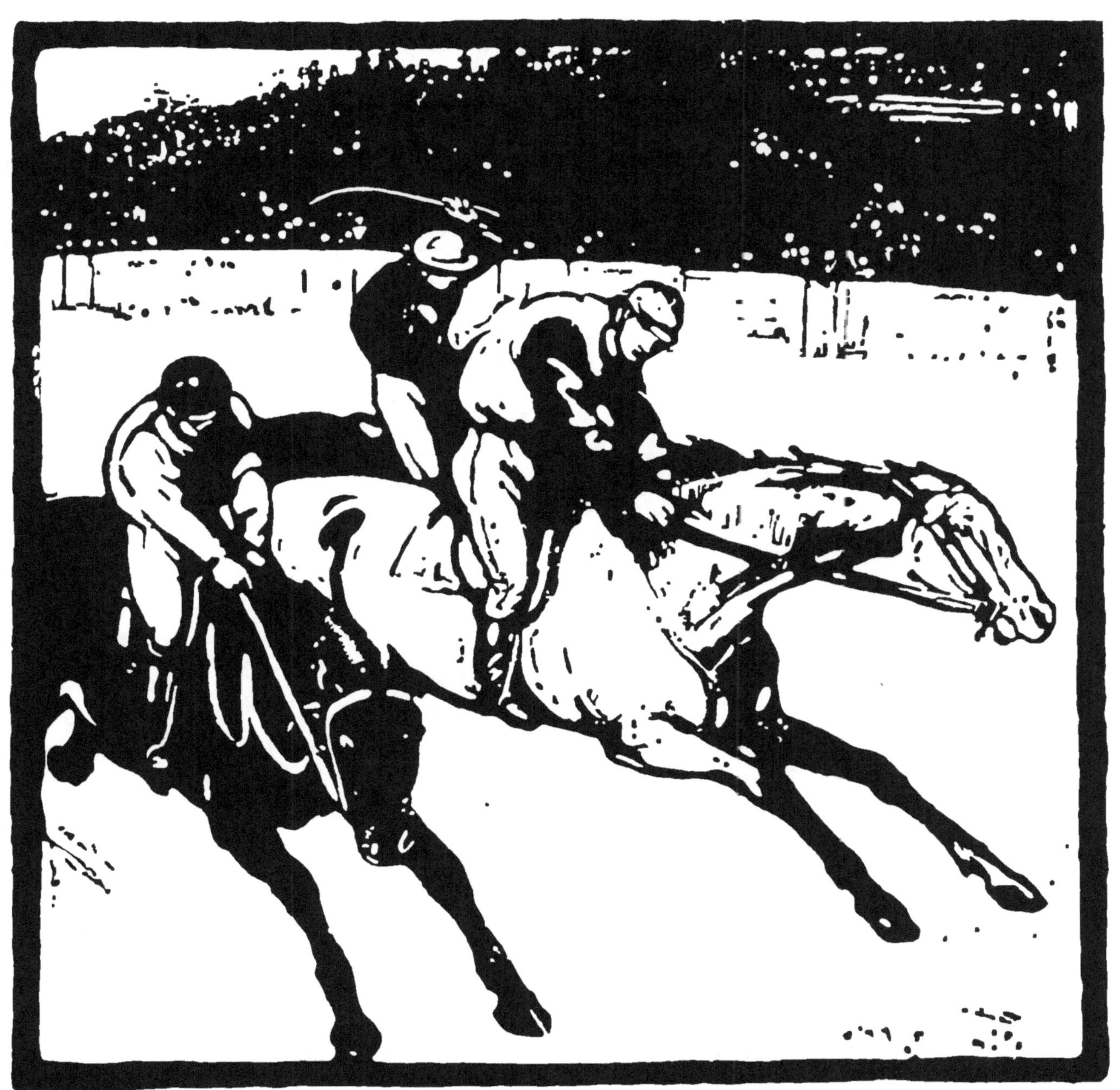

March.

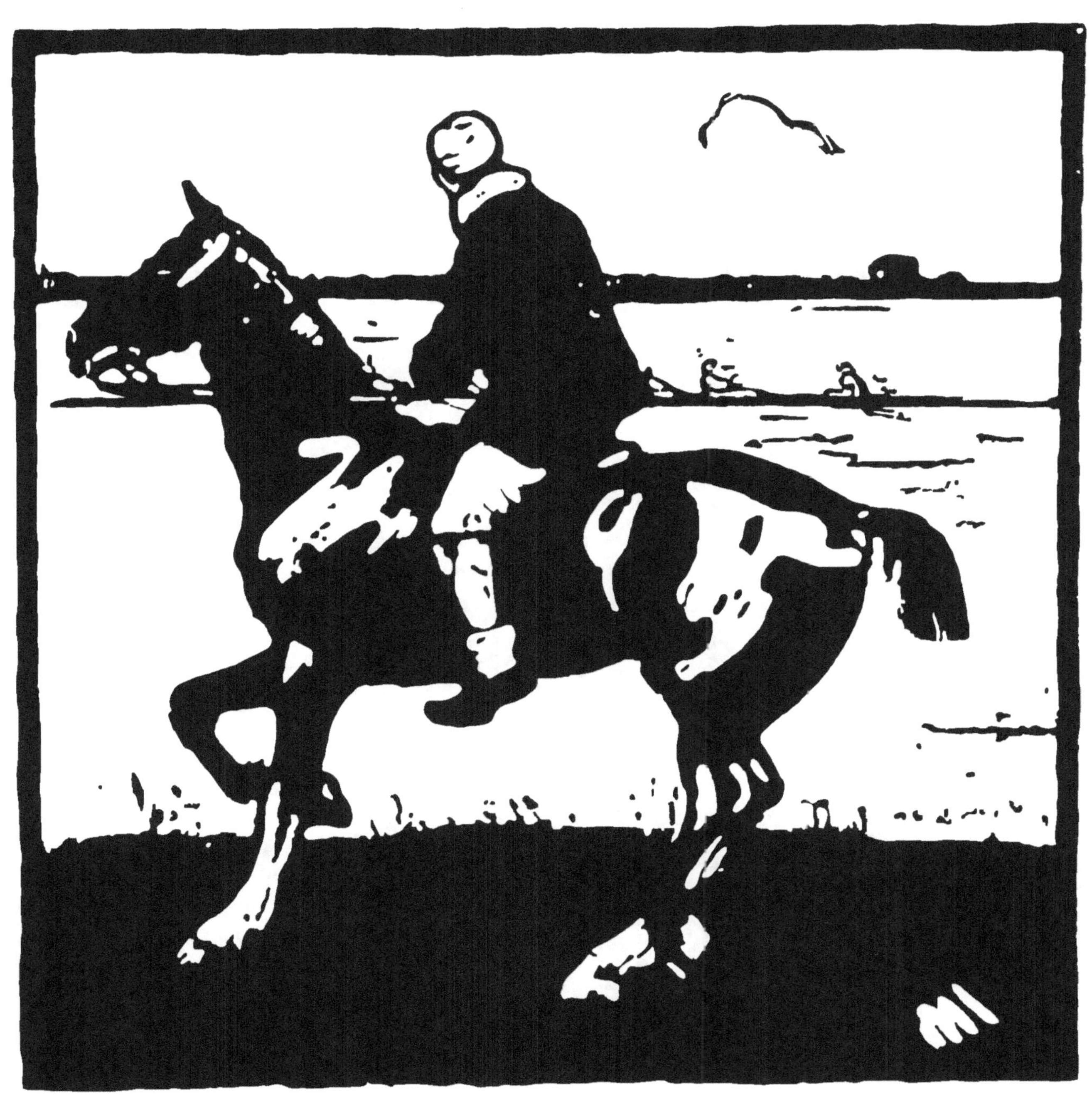

April.

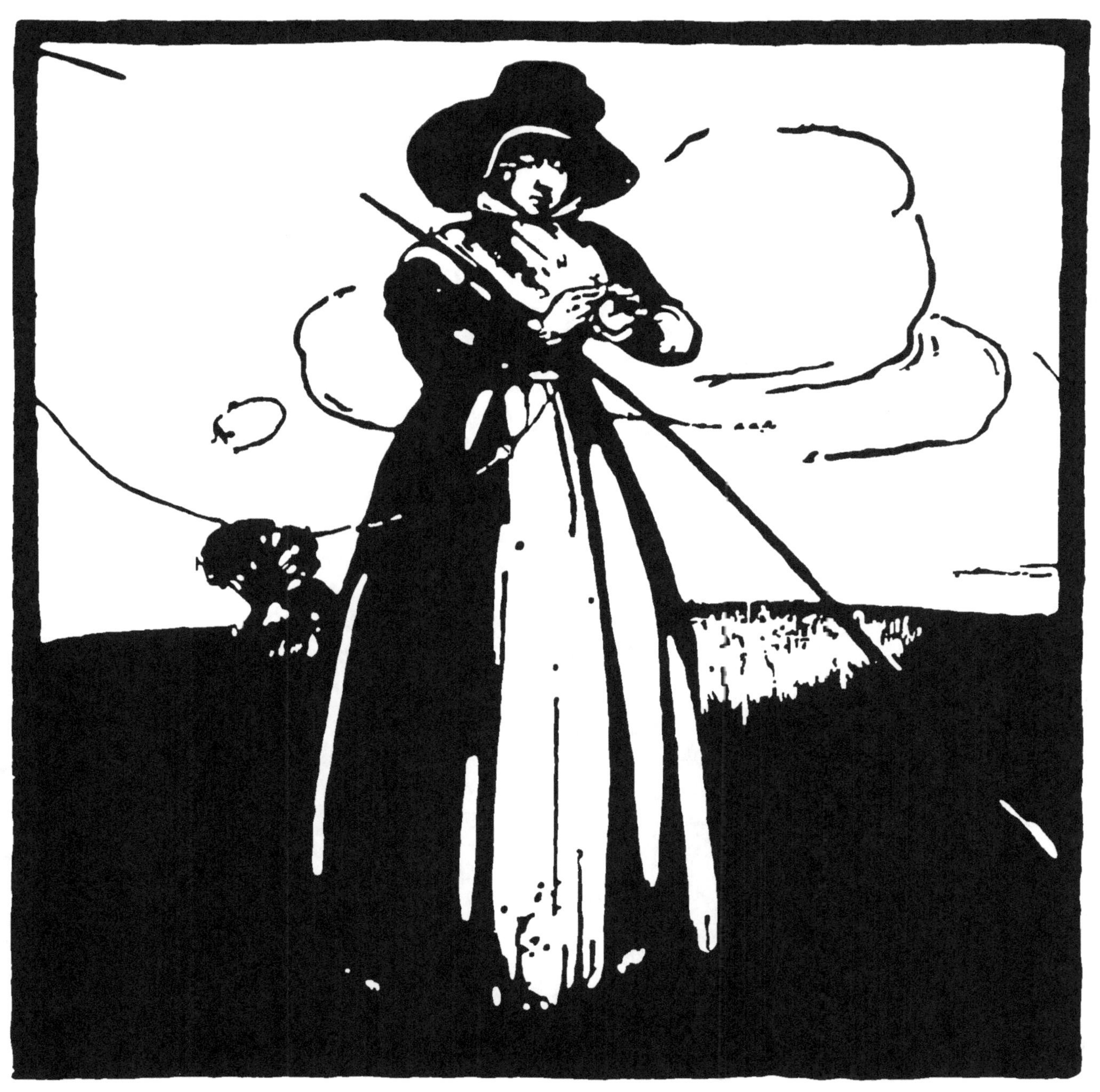

May.

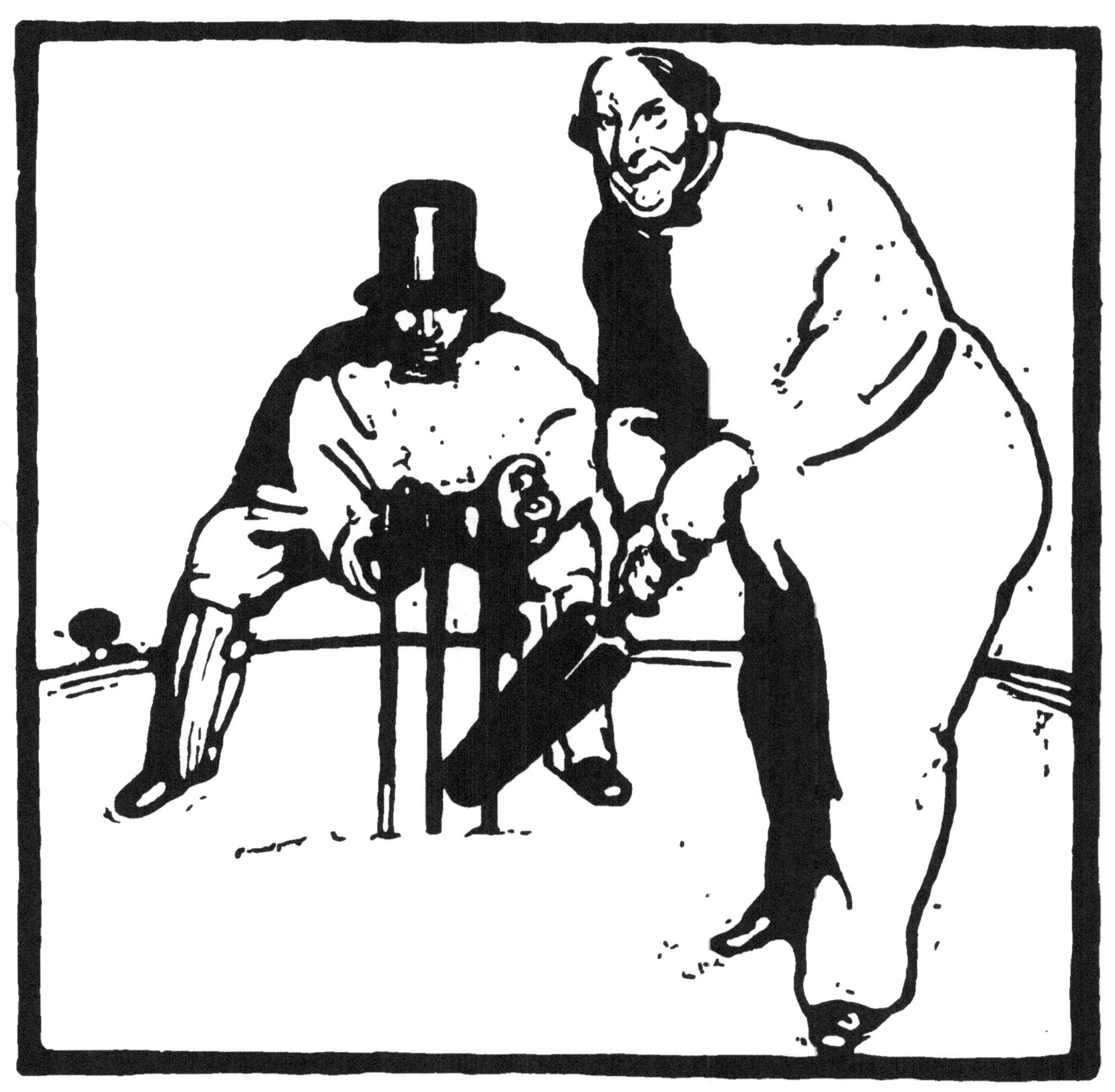

June.

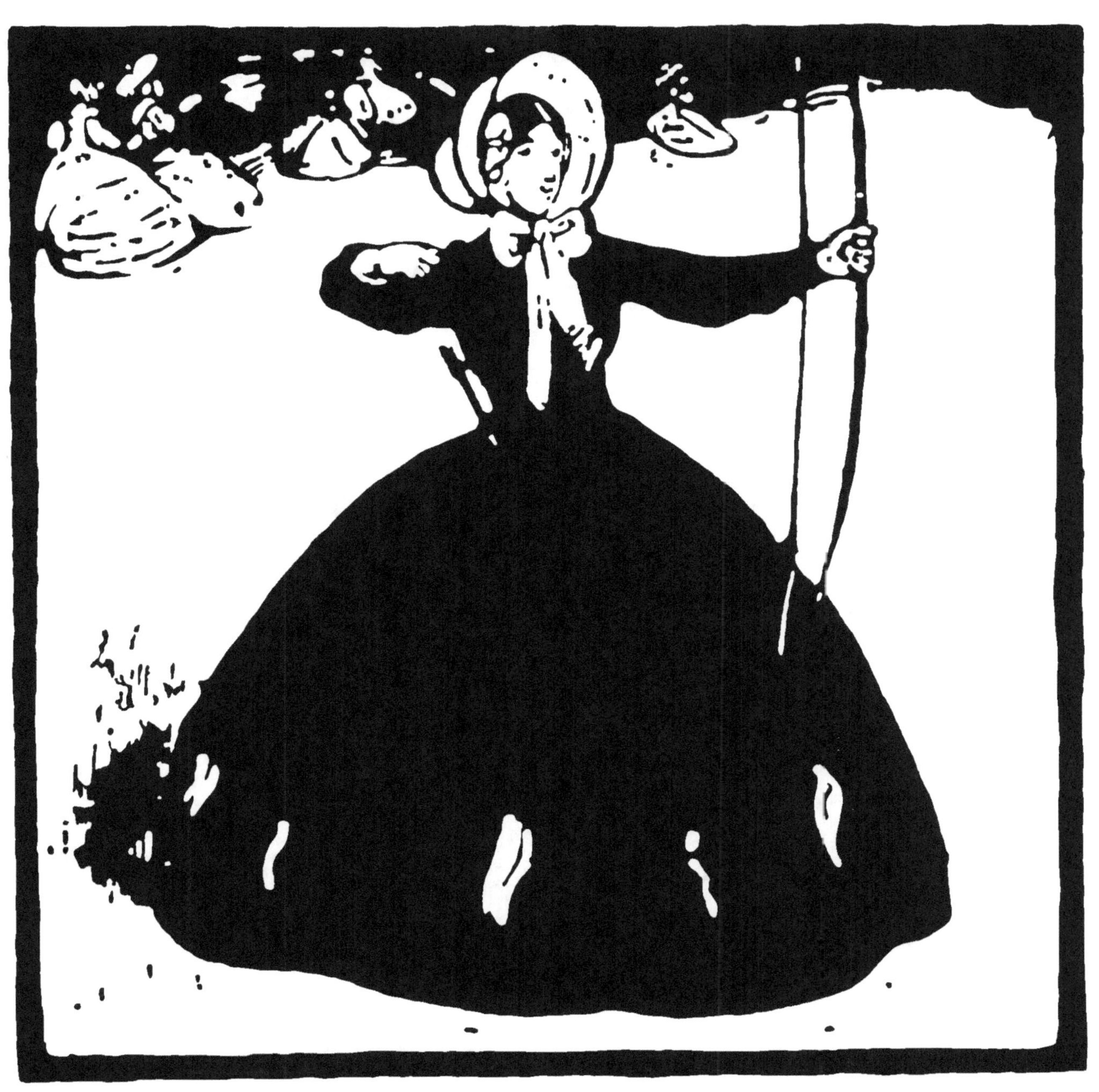

July.

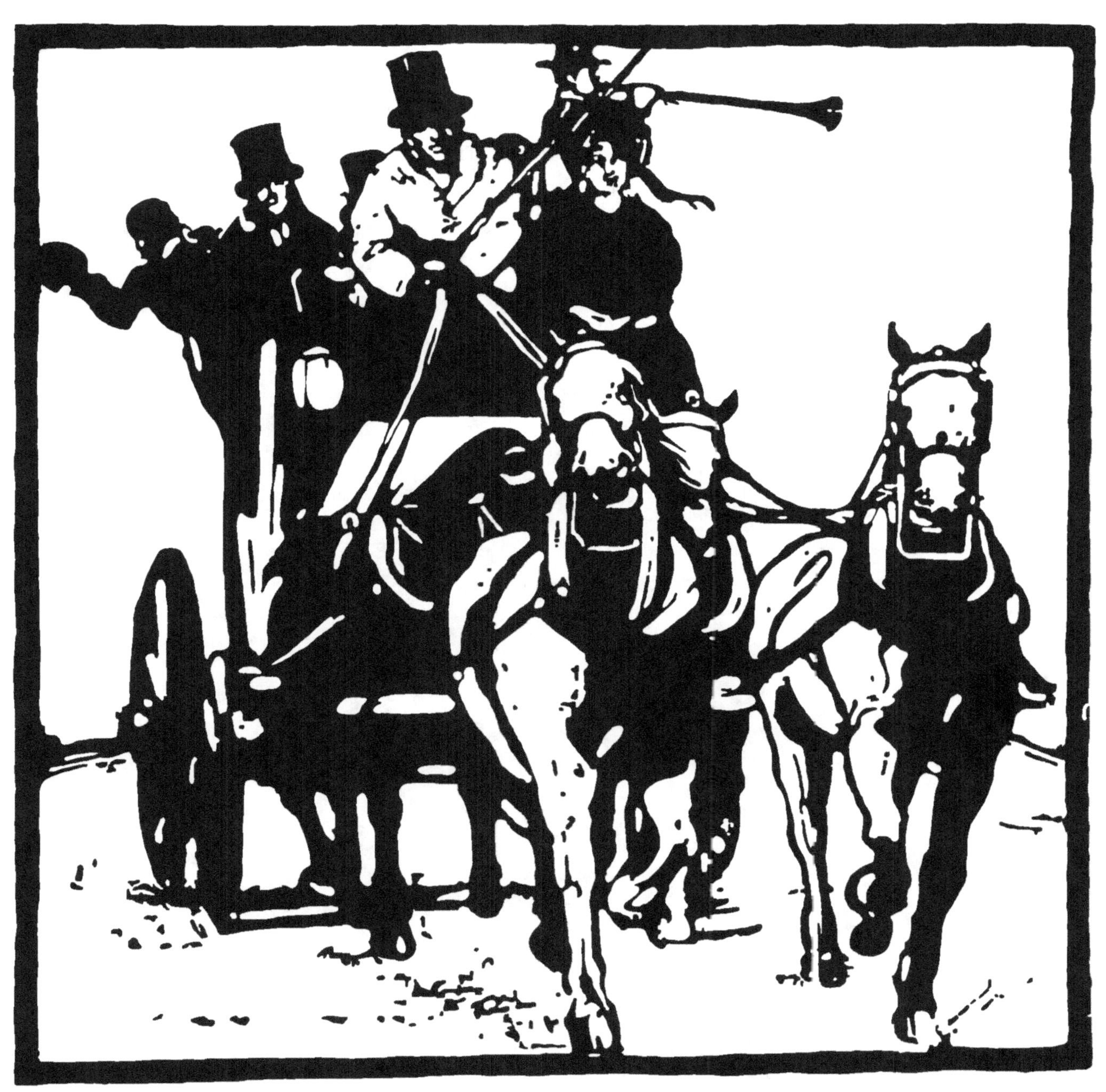

August.

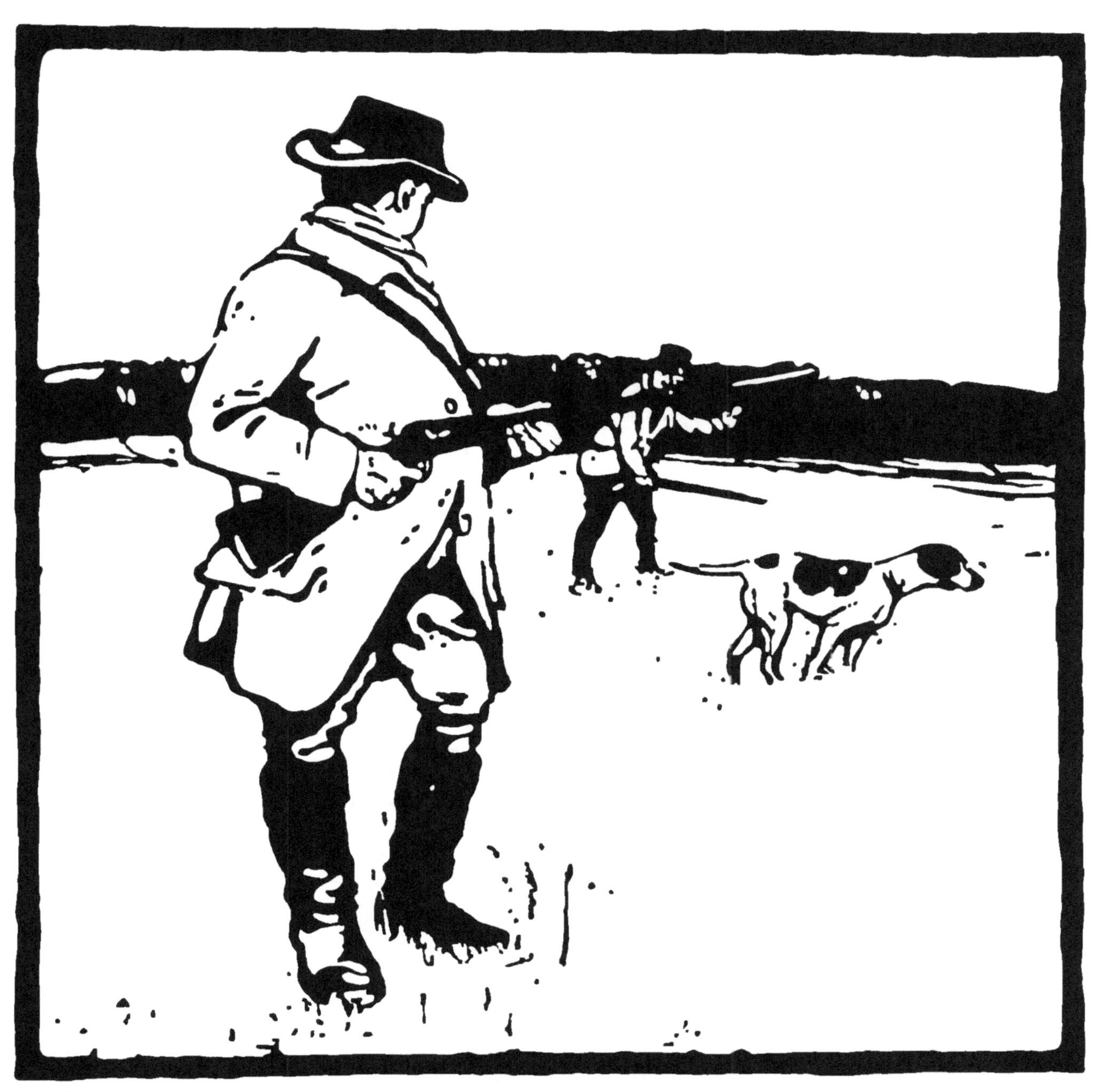

September.

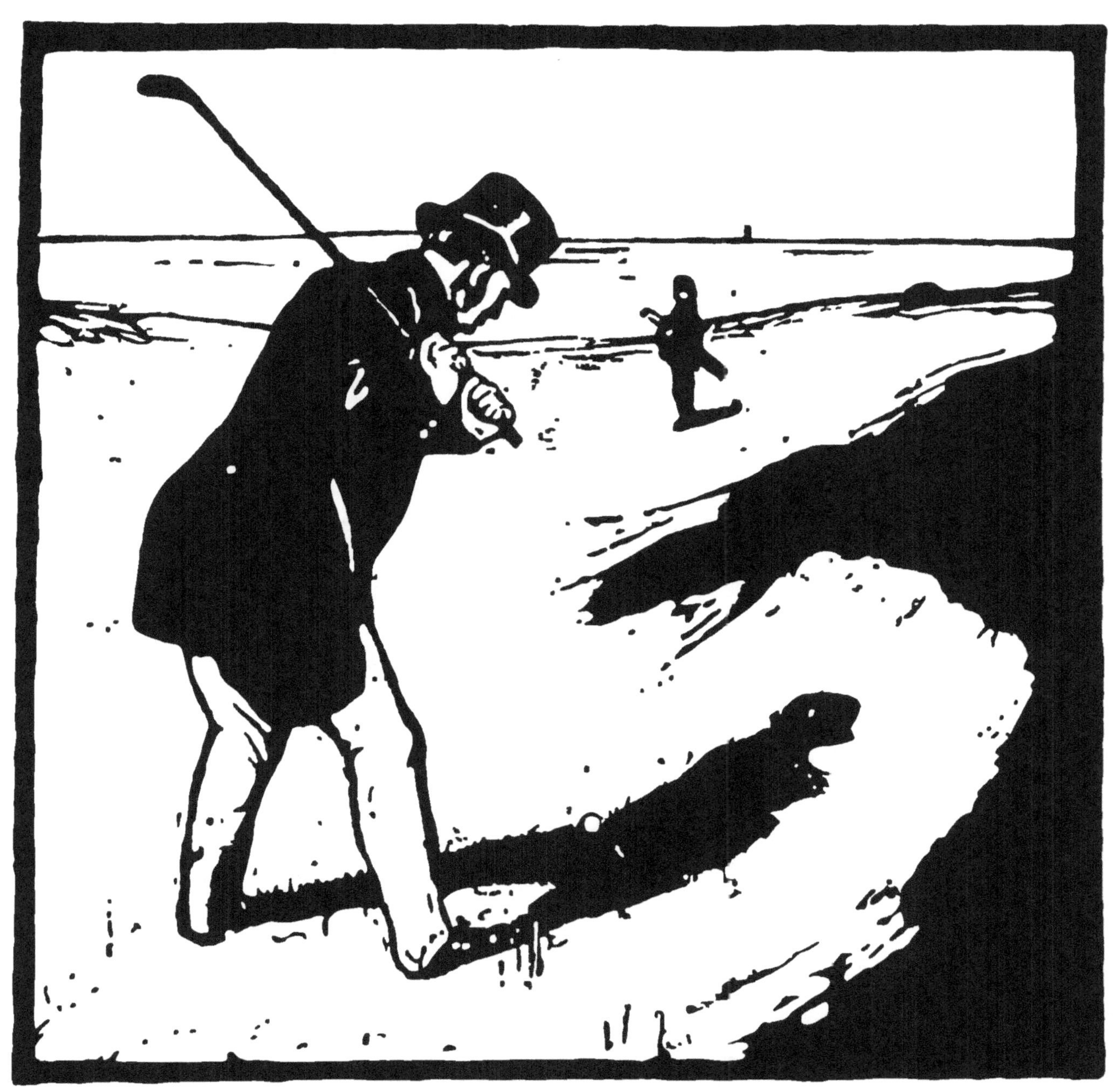

October.

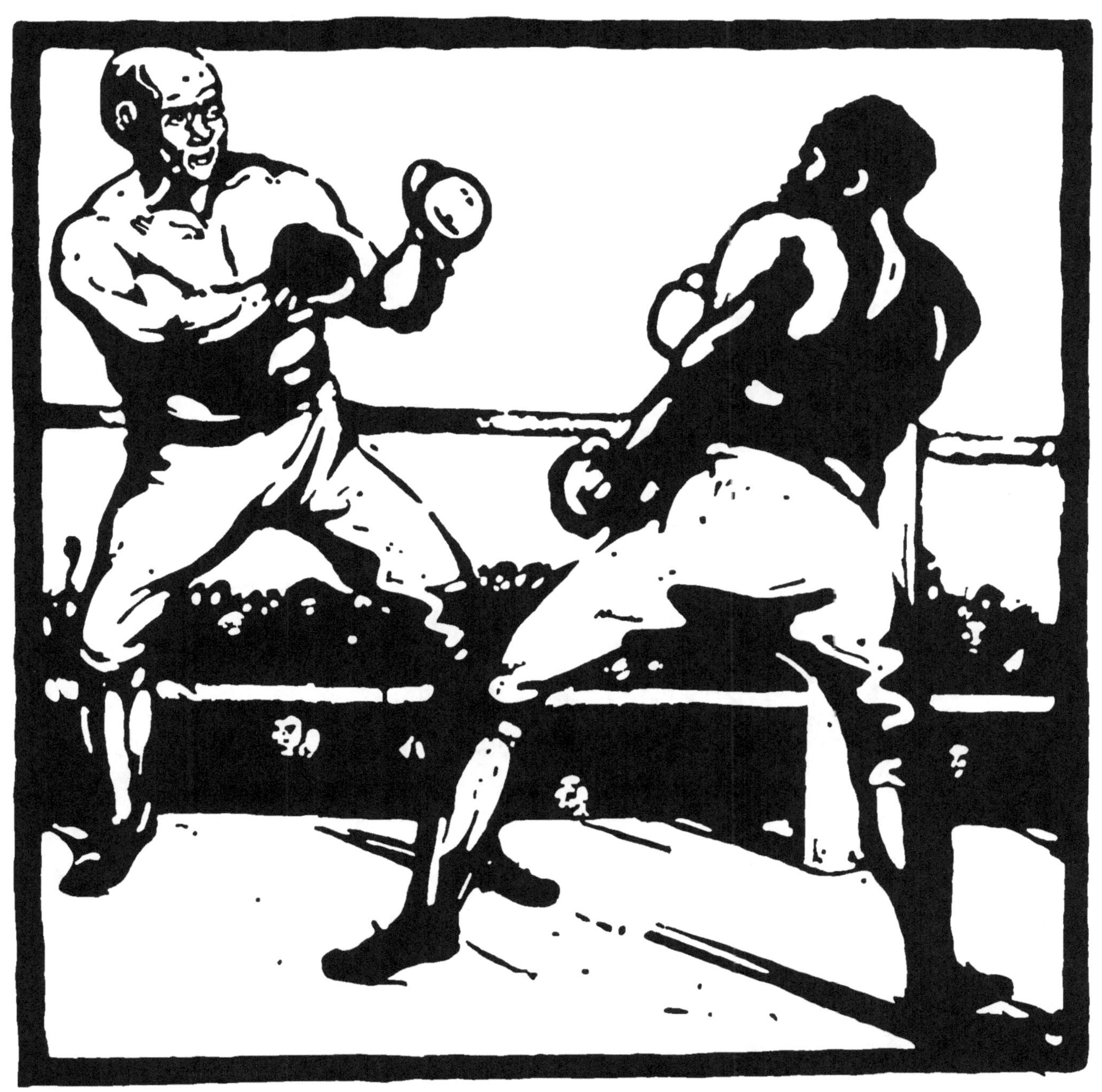

November.

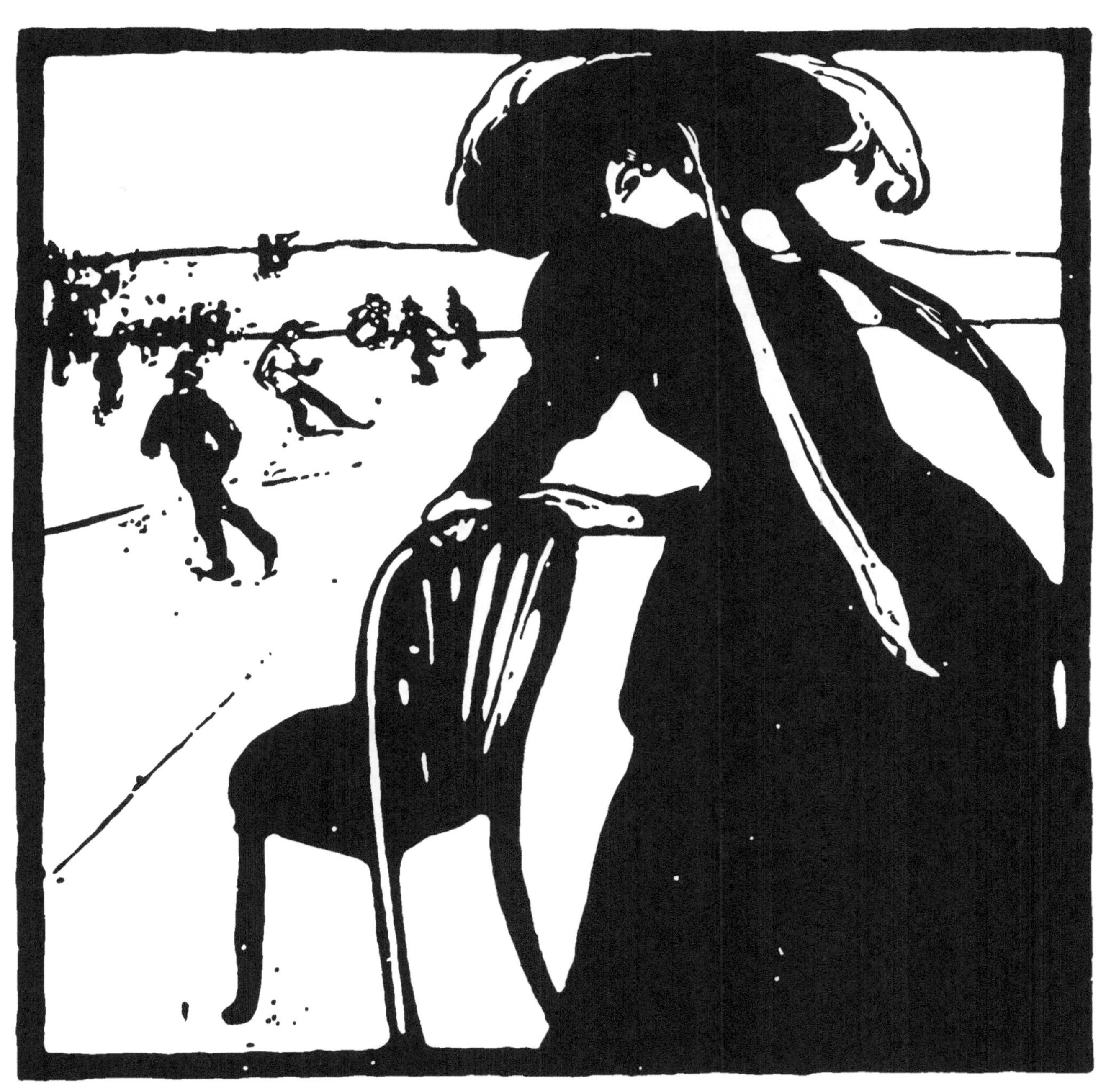

December.

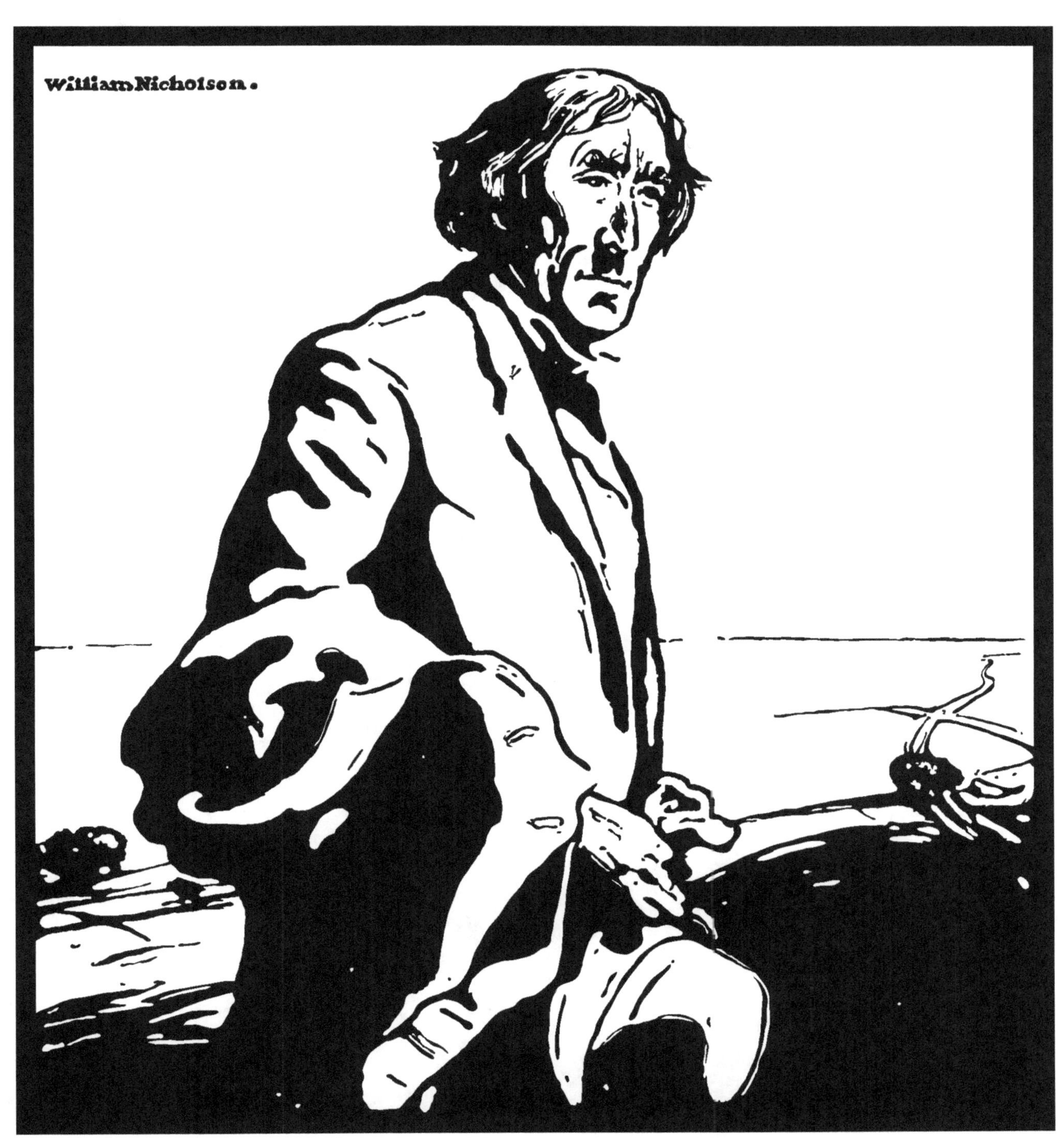

Sir Henry Irving.

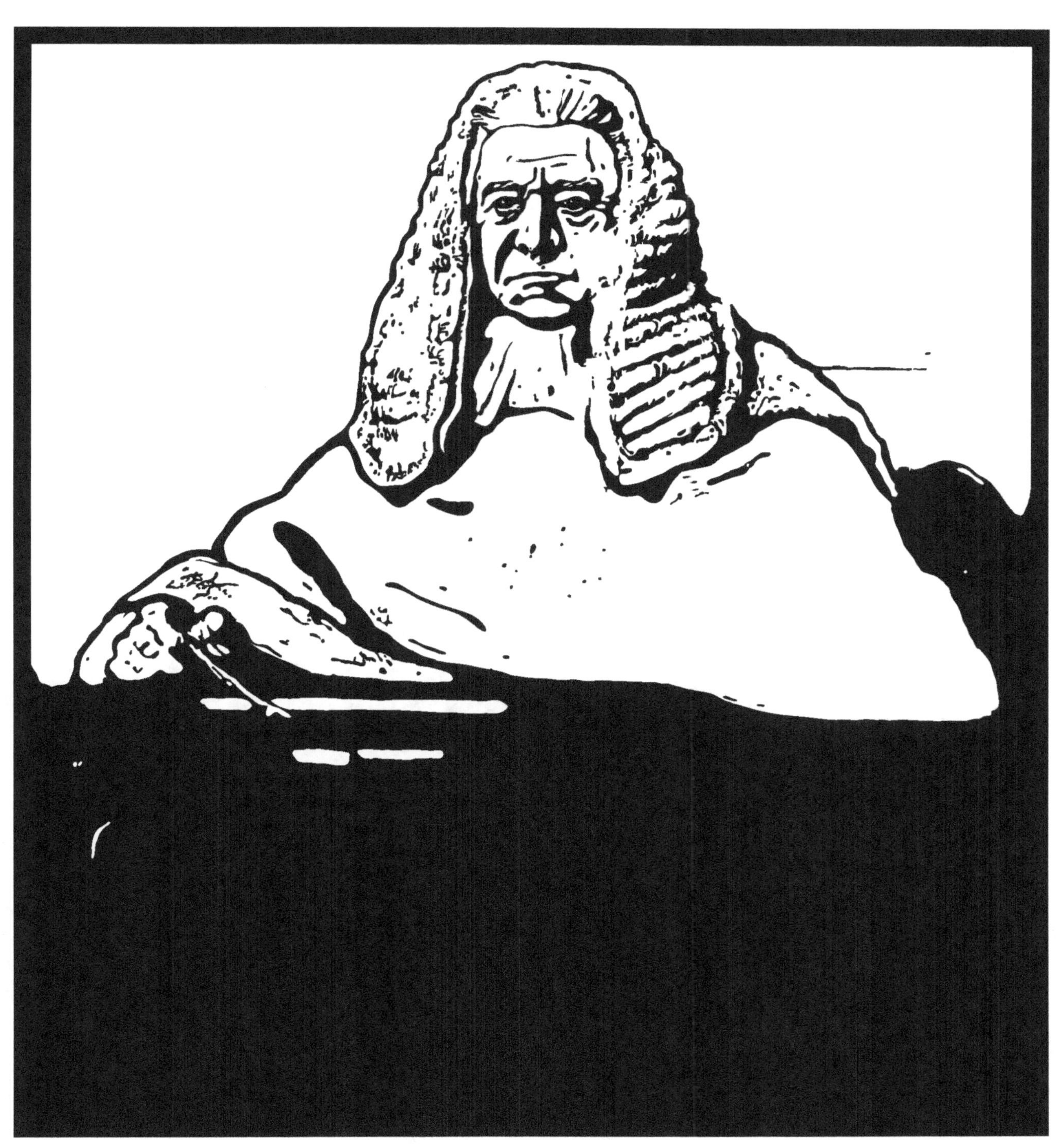

Sir Henry Hawkins.

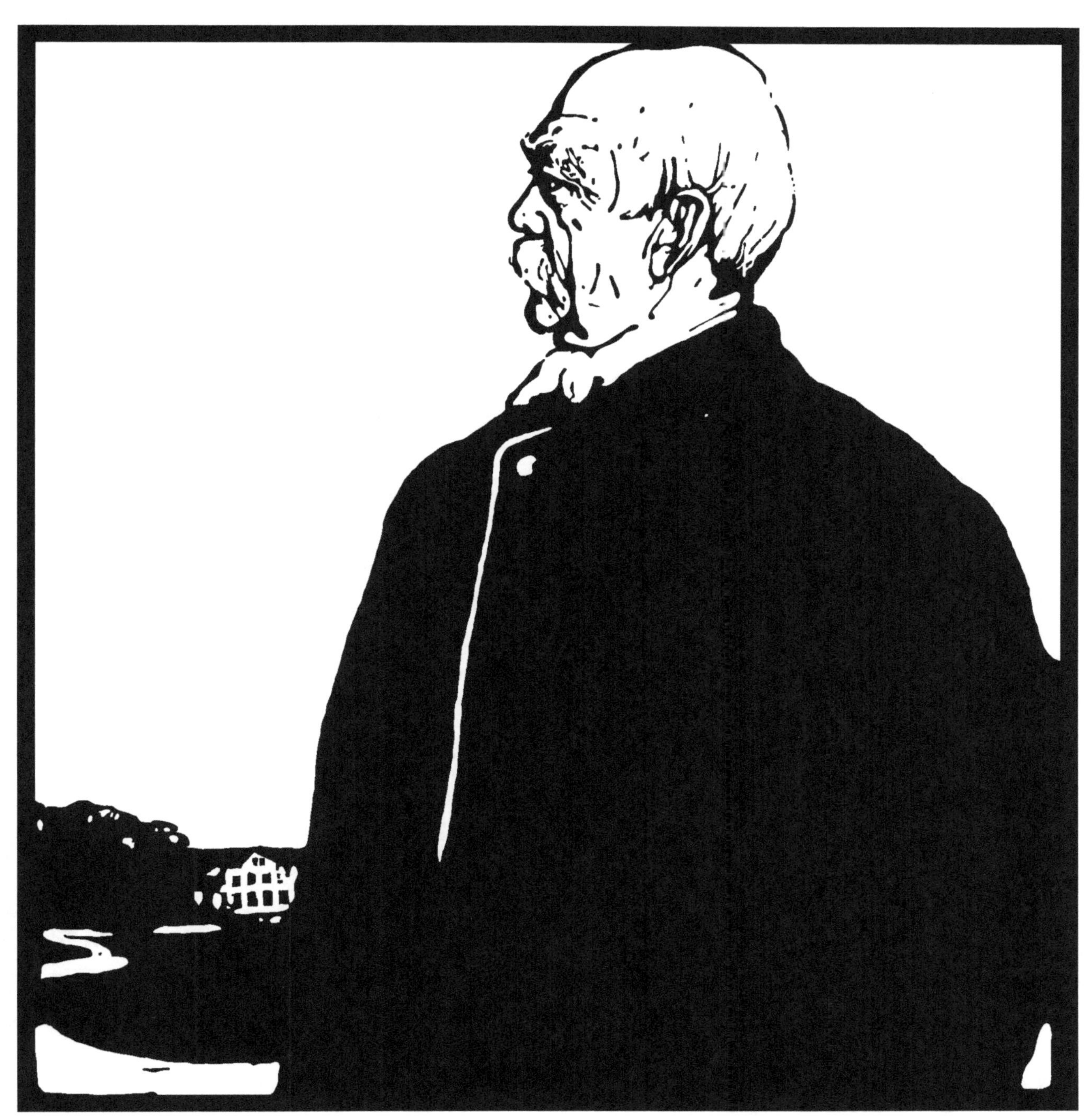

Prince Bismarck.

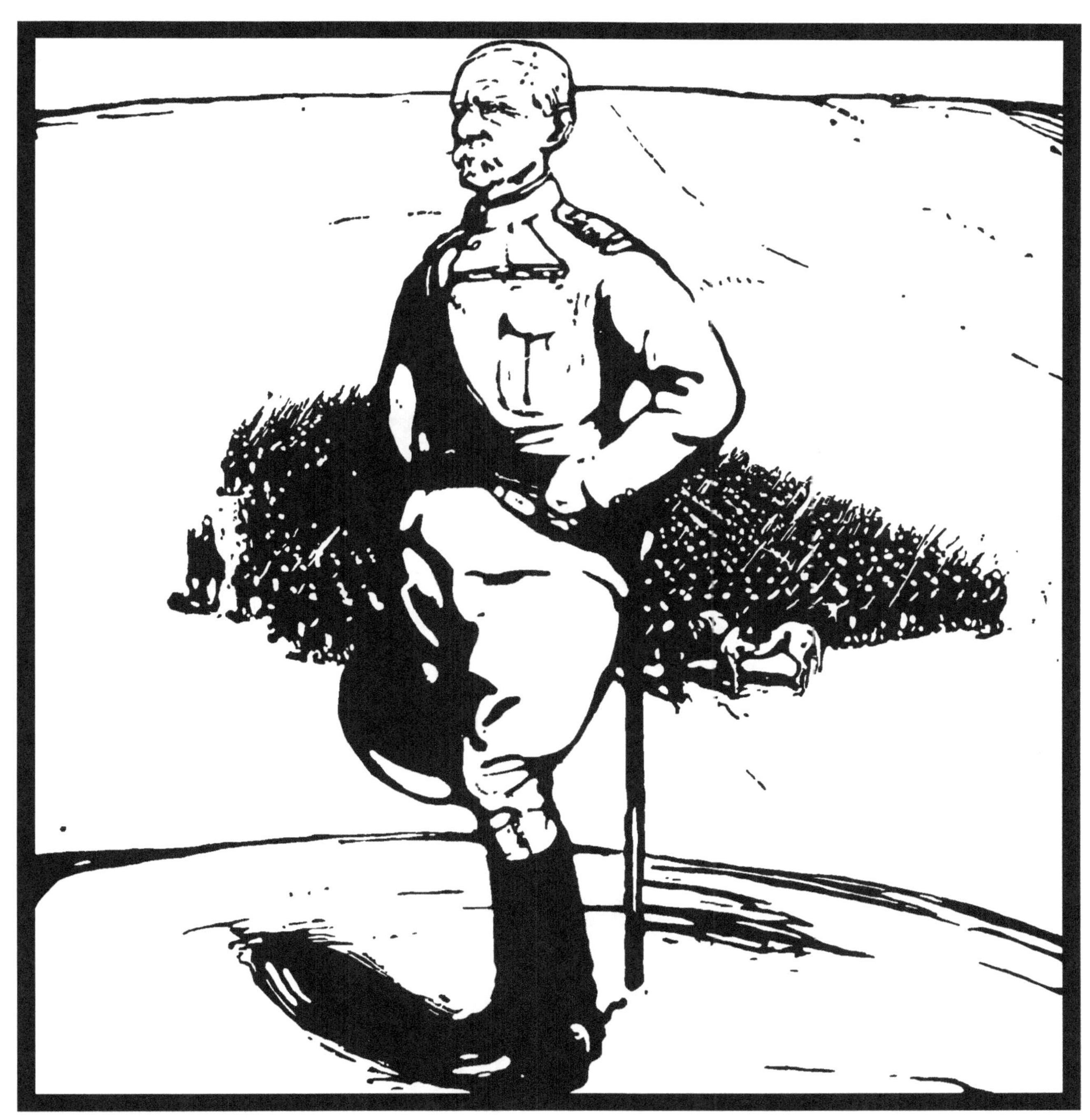

Lord Roberts.

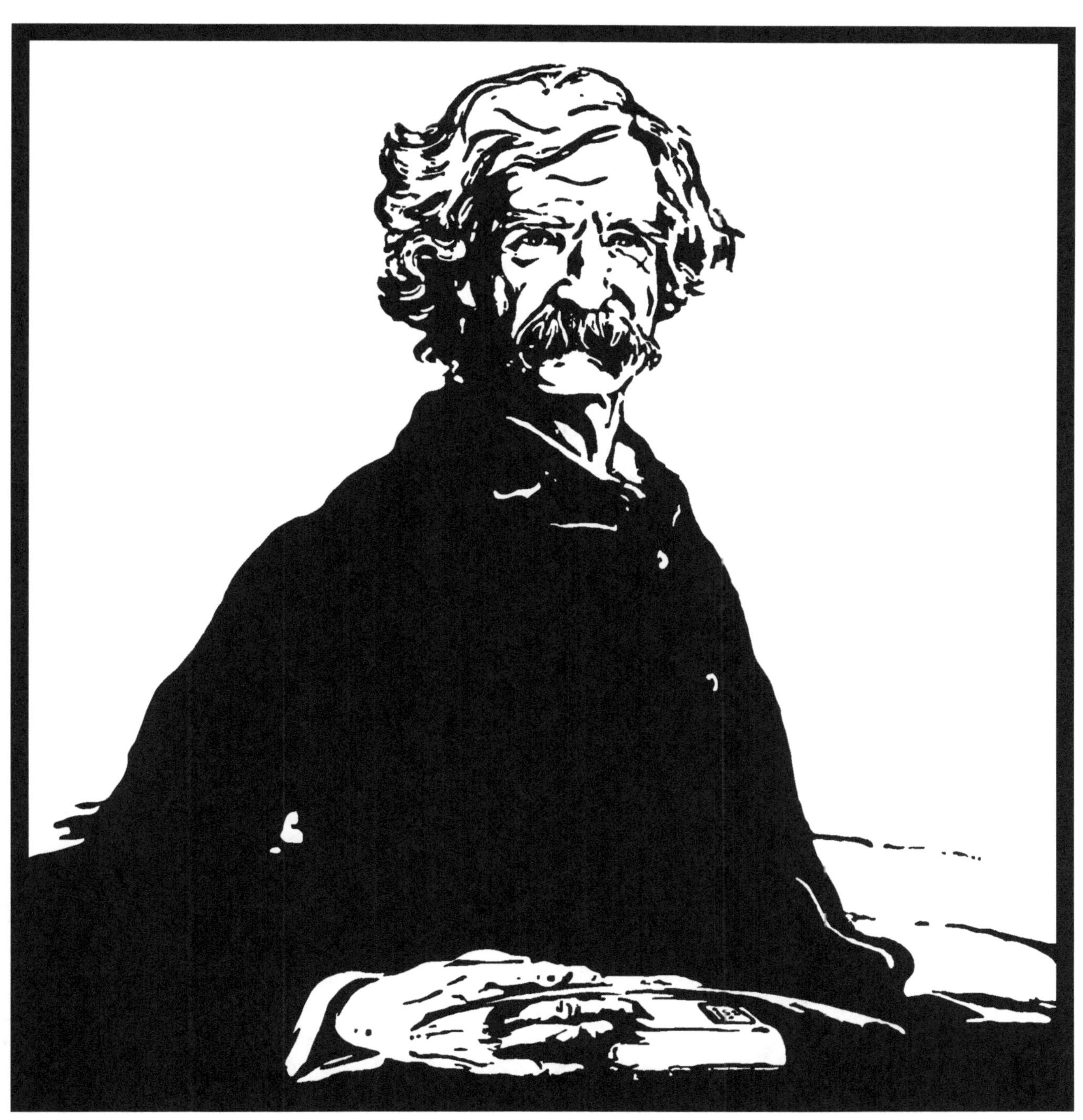

Mark Twain

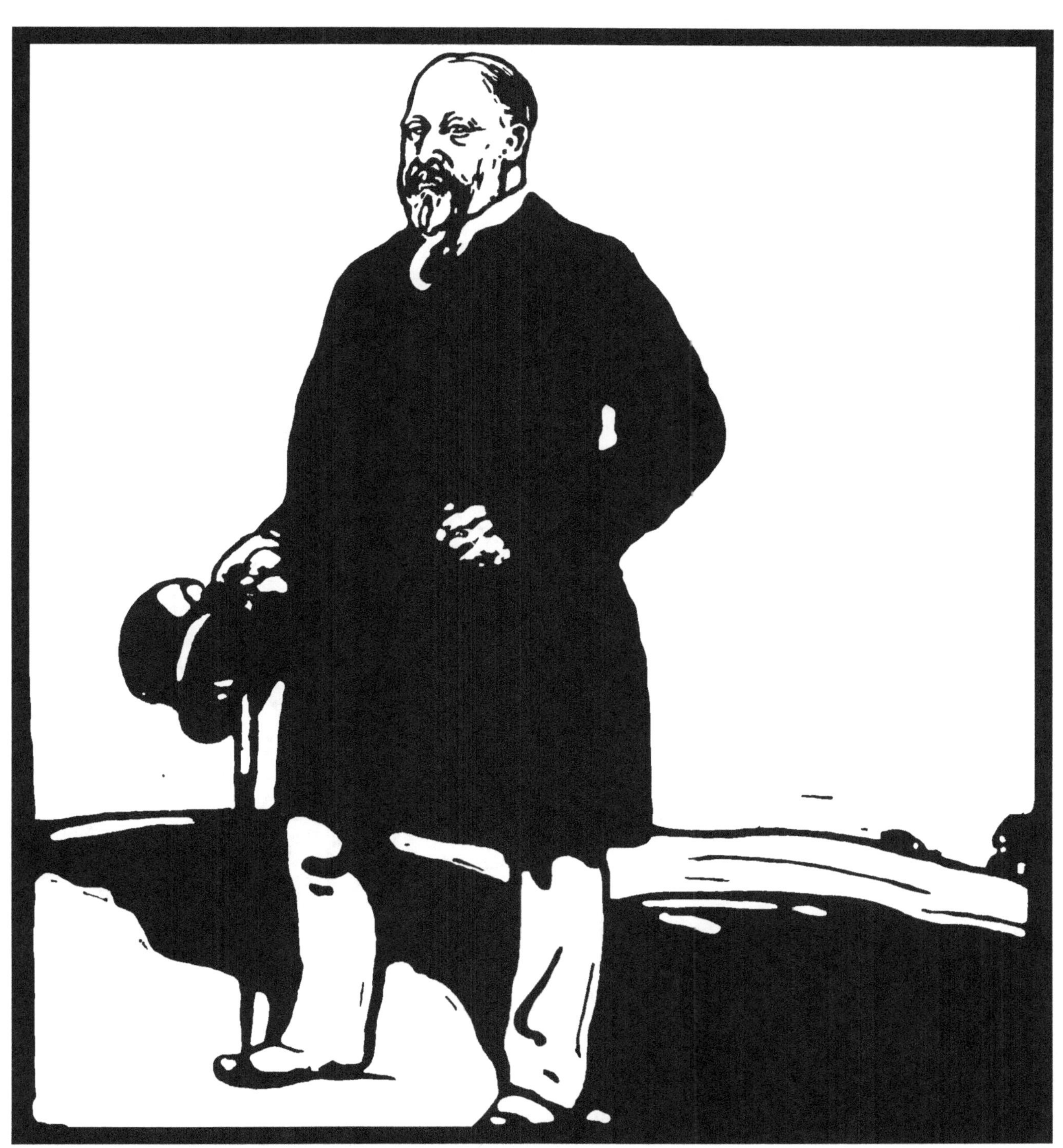

H.R.H.The Prince of Wales.

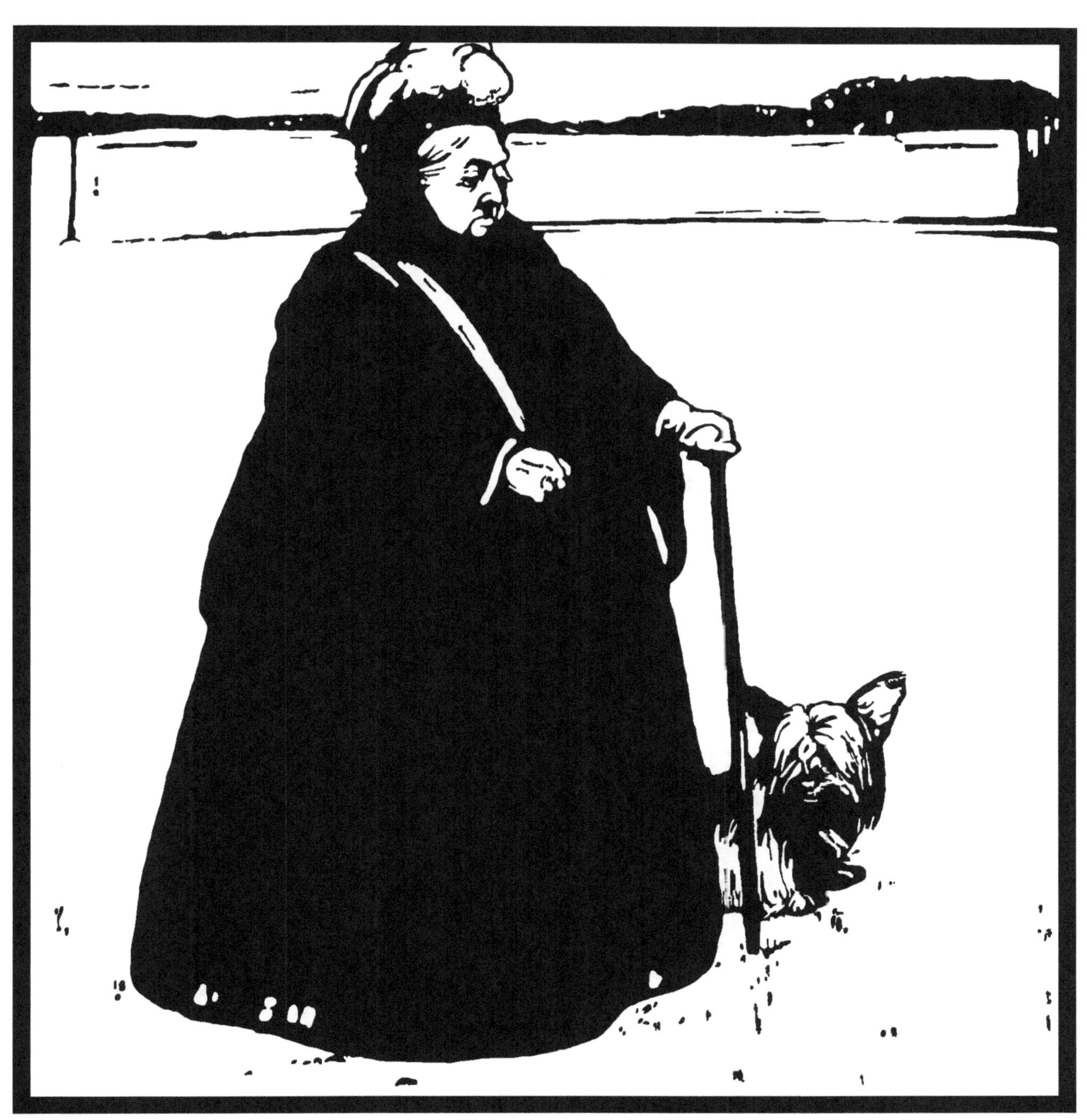

H.M.The Queen.

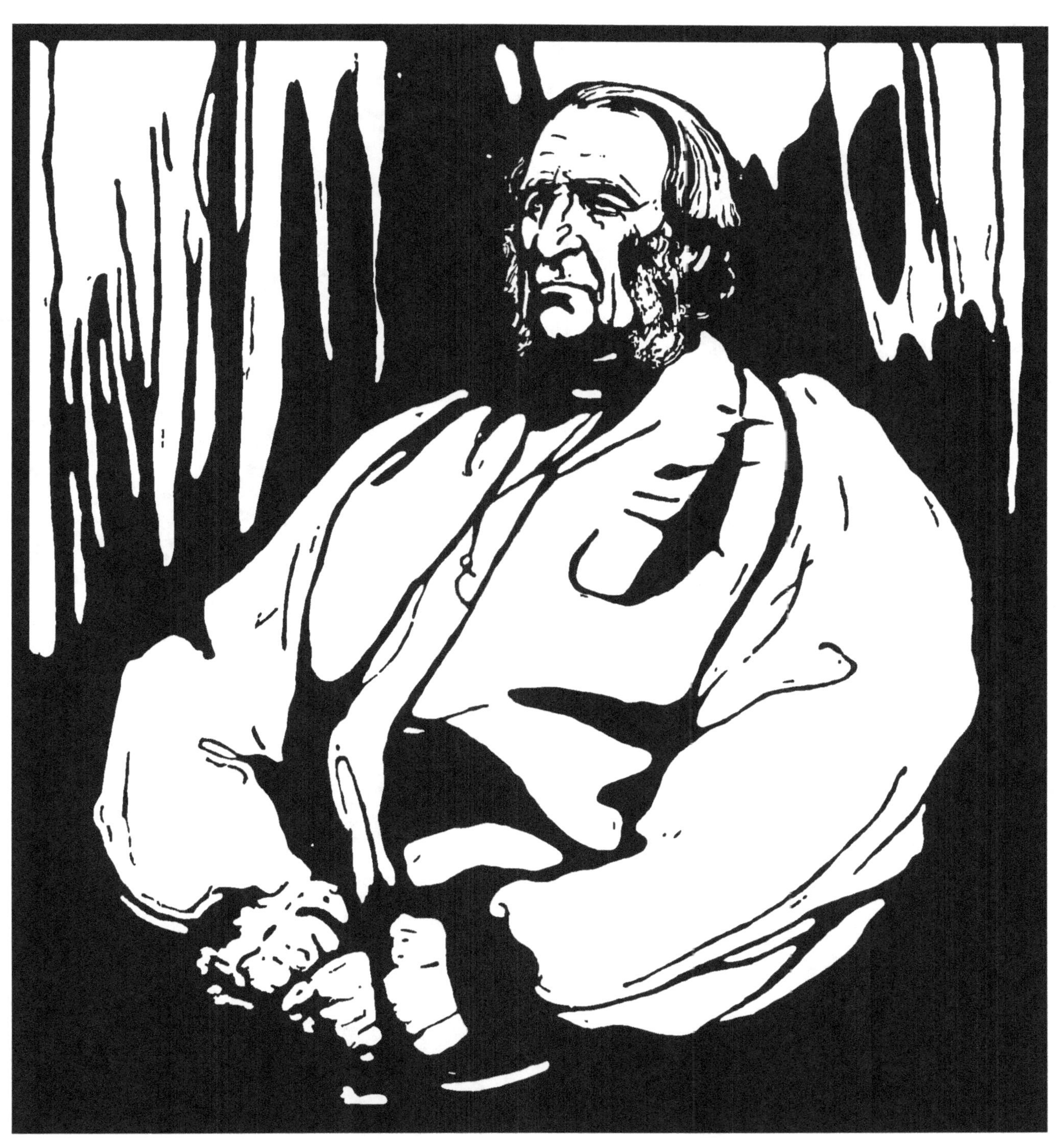

The Archbishop of Canterbury.

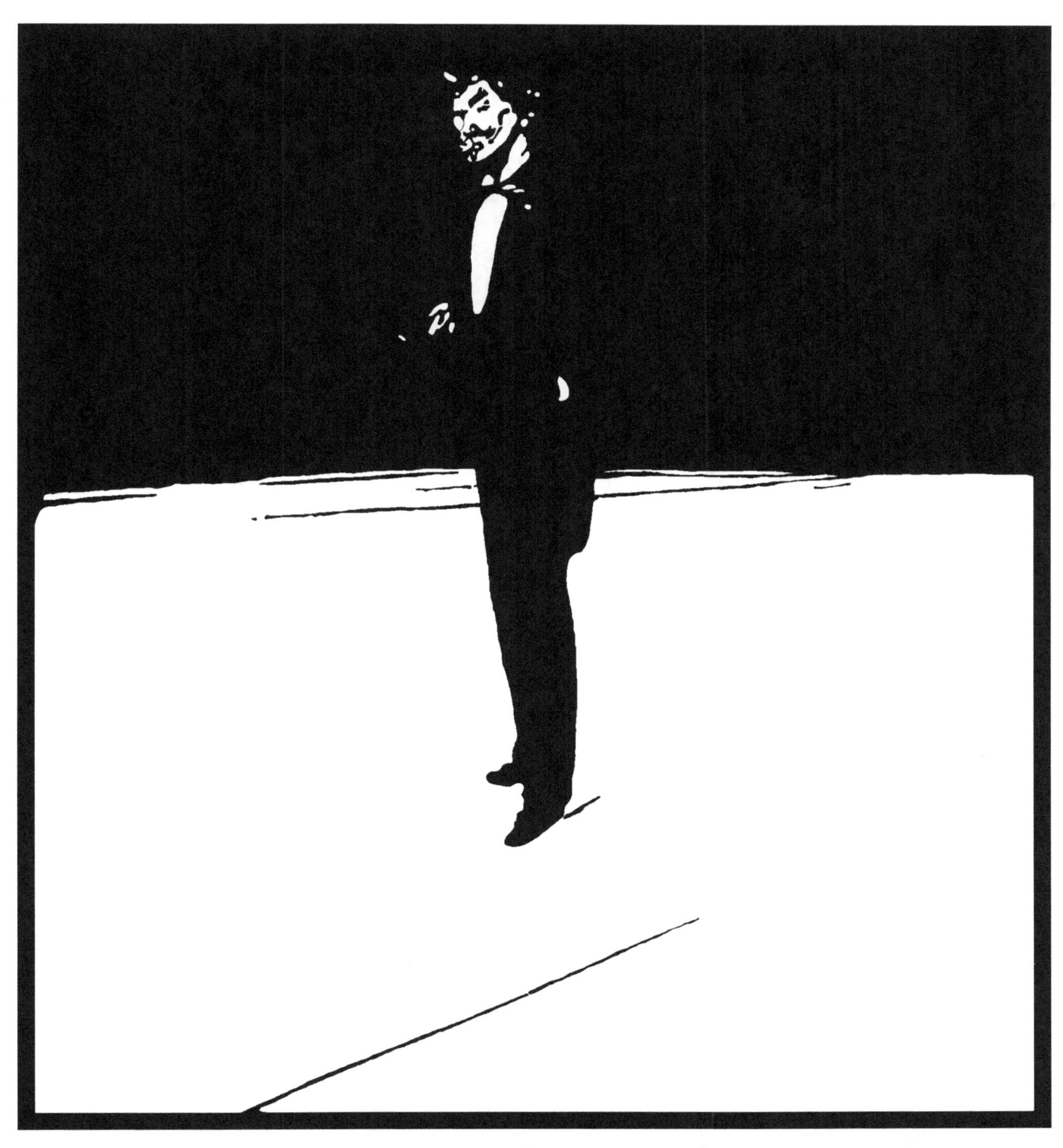

James McNeill Whistler.

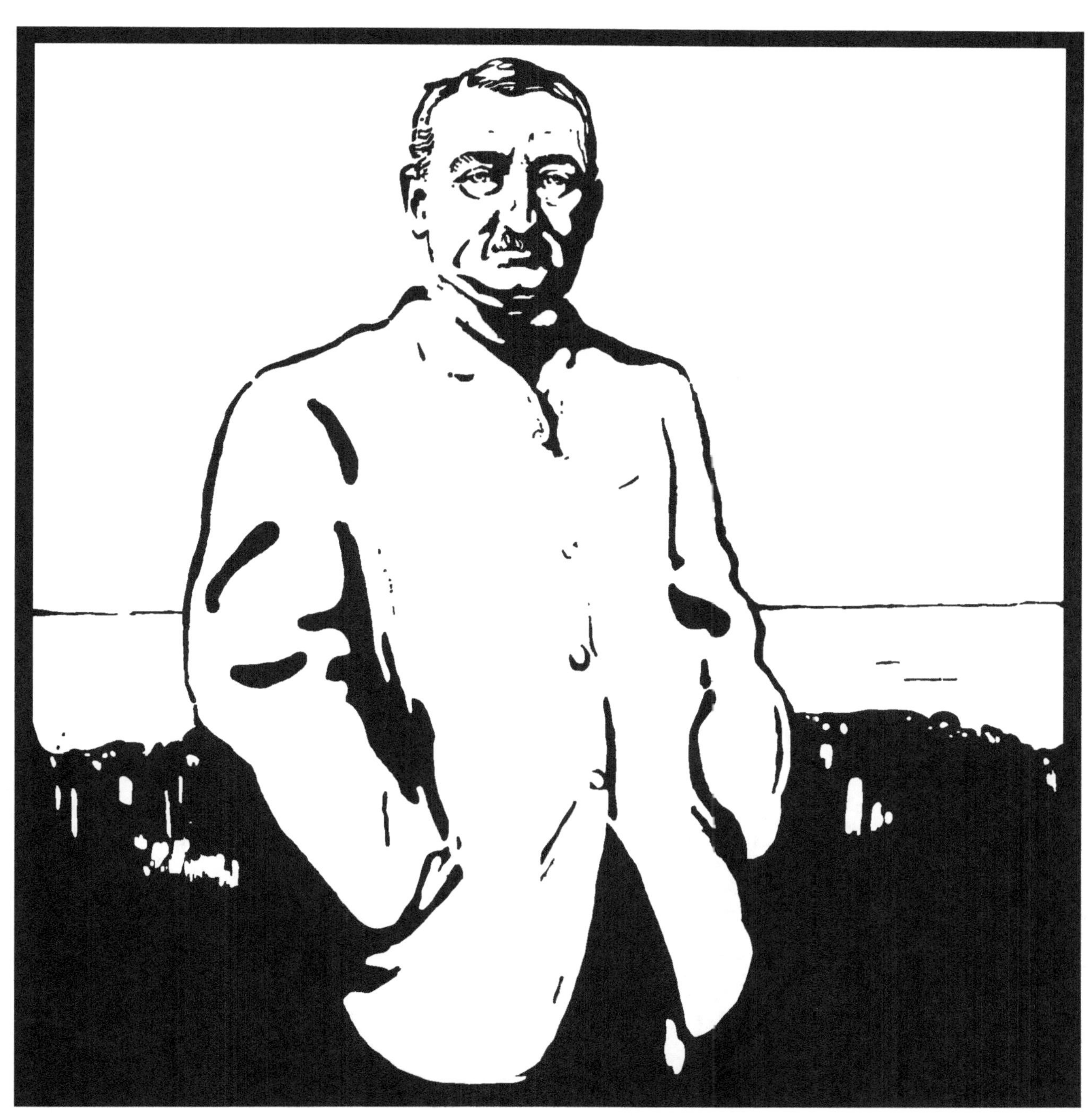

Cecil Rhodes.

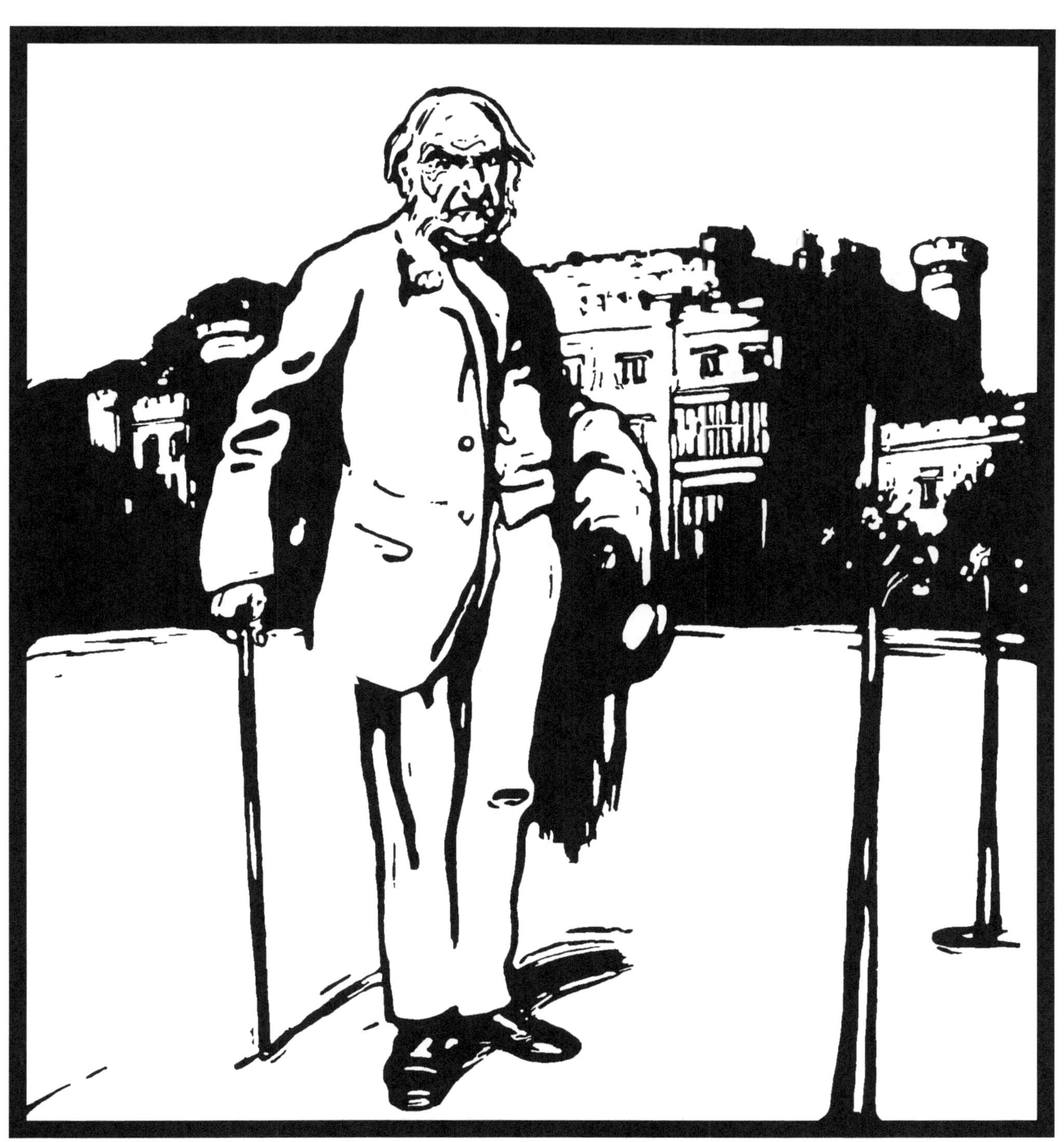

W. E. Gladstone.

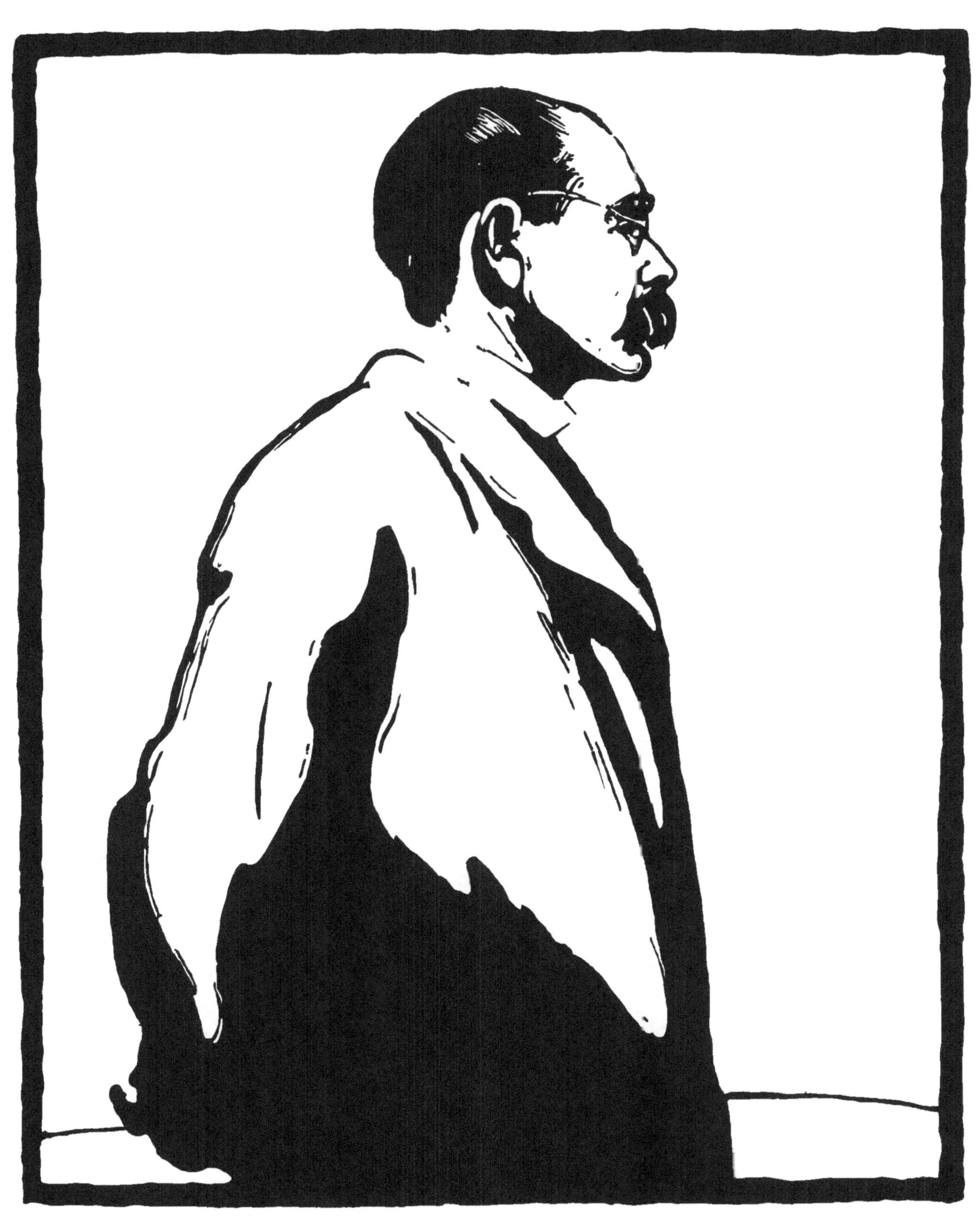

Rudyard Kipling.

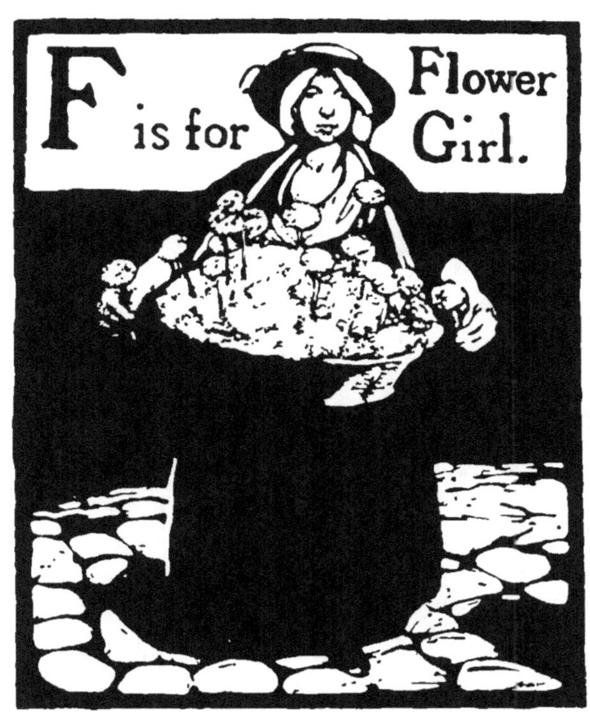

If you have enjoyed this book, please look out for the following title:

An Alphabet by William Nicholson

from Velluminous Press.